THIS CLOSE
TO THE EARTH

THIS CLOSE
TO THE EARTH

Enid Shomer

The University of Arkansas Press
Fayetteville 1992

96   95   94   93   92   5   4   3   2   1

This book was designed by Gail Carter using the typefaces Berkeley and Charlemagne.

The paper used in this publication meets the minimum requirements of the
American National Standard for Permanence of Paper for Printed Library
Materials Z39.48-1984. ∞

Library of Congress Cataloging-in-Publication Data

Shomer, Enid.
    This close to the earth / Enid Shomer.
        p.   cm.
    ISBN 1-55728-255-2 (alk. paper). — ISBN 1-55728-256-0 (pbk. : alk. paper)
    I. Title.
PS3569.H5783T47   1992
811'.54--dc20   91-45530
                                                                        CIP

Acknowledgments

I am grateful to the National Endowment for the Arts and the Florida Arts Council for fellowships which helped to support me during the writing of some of these poems, and to the Virginia Center for the Creative Arts.

My thanks to the editors of the following publications in which these poems first appeared: *ARETE: Forum for Thought; Iowa Woman; Kalliope; The Madison Review; The Massachusetts Review; Midstream; The New Criterion; The Paris Review; Ploughshares; The Tampa Review;* and *Tikkun.*

The following poems first appeared in *Poetry,* copyright 1988, 1989, 1990, 1991, and 1992 by The Modern Poetry Association: "Villa Maria"; "For Those Who Are No Longer Young"; "Romantic, at Horseshoe Key"; "The Last Father Poem"; "Reading a Violent Love Poem to the Deaf"; "The Suit Too Small, the Words"; and all of "Pope Joan."

"The Uncommon Hours" was first published in a different form in my chapbook *Florida Postcards* (1987, Winner of the Jubilee Press Chapbook Competition).

"Sestina for Indian Summer" won the 1989 Celia B. Wagner Award of the Poetry Society of America and first appeared in the *Poetry Society of America Newsletter.*

"Fishing Seahorse Reef" is included in the *1989 Anthology of Magazine Verse & Yearbook of American Poetry.*

"Learning CPR" was awarded the 1992 Wildwood Prize in poetry and first appeared in *The Wildwood Journal.*

A special thanks to Peg Libertus for her help.

Contents

III

I

Fishing Seahorse Reef

Our lures trail
in the prop-wash,
skipping to mimic
live bait. Minutes ago
I watched you
cut up the dead shrimp
that smell like sex.
Now we stand, long
filmy shapes jigsawed
by the waves, and wait
for the rods to arc
heavy with kingfish.
We bring the limit
of eight on board,
their teeth gnashing
against the lures.
And I think how tender
all animal urgency is—
these fish thrashing
to throw the hook,
or a man flinging himself
into the future
each time he enters
a woman. This
is what I picture
all afternoon: you
inside me, your body a stem

bent under the weight
of its flowering,
as beautiful as that;
how carefully
you would lower yourself,
like something winged,
a separate order
of fallen thing
from these angels with fins
who know only once
the difference
between water and air.

For Those Who Are No Longer Young

My mother believed we are all kind
but some lack the chance to prove it.
She organized rummage sales.
One year the washer flooded, waterlogging
all the donated clothes in our basement.
She showed me pictures of orphans,
their glazed eyes reflecting whatever
I wished: famine, a smoking car wreck
which only they survived. She made
hospital calls but never said *breast*
or *cancer*. They opened Mrs. Silverman
like a melon but sewed her right up,
her insides strangling with it
like a foundation cracked by tree roots.
I hung the soggy hand-me-downs out to dry—
madras shirts bled pale and limp,
the wool coat in which some man would cross
a street not knowing it was the last day
of his life, like Marie Curie's husband,
Pierre, crushed by a wagon wheel.
Over and over I read how she gathered up
bits of his brain and skull
and kept them hidden in a scarf
like a broken strand of rosary beads. . . .
             And before that,
the habit of bravery in her garret
where she fainted dead away from a diet

4

of radishes and tea. Later, the vials
of radioactive salts glowed in the dark,
contaminating even the notebooks
where she and Pierre wrote *we propose
to call it* polonium *from the name
of the original country of one of us.*

If my mother was deceived, if kindness
is only the fear of evil,
I did not know it that night I lay
on the warm slate roof above our den
smelling the Seckle pear blooms,
waiting for the constellations to appear.
I feared her kindness,
all her kept promises. Below me, in the house,
she pressed dignity back into old clothes.
That day all she could do was watch
Mrs. Silverman sleep, her body grown light,
already lifting to take its place
in the open grave of the sky
with the others whose names I knew—
the Pleiades, burning with grief
for Atlas, Andromeda, once offered
as a sacrifice, and her mother,
Cassiopeia, the Lady in the Chair.

Reading a Violent Love Poem to the Deaf

I imagine it's asters the signer
is clenching, their dense centers

long vowels, each a boutonniere
she plants in our lapels.

Delay is what connects me to her—
a lag between speech and gesture

as formal and stately as velvet festoons.
Delay is everything the air burns with,

each crook of her finger
a diacritical spark. I'm seeing legerdemain;

they're seeing American Sign,
a language held like an intricate fan

before the face, but less deceptive.
In the stabbing she mimics, motive

comes clear, the signs cascading
onto the retina so that her song,

drawn on the air, bears its own history,
the love before the knife a wispy

skywriting dissolving before our eyes.
My own hands, clown-sized saboteurs,

betray me with sub-text, as if even
years after I've written these lines

I might reach again for knives
instead of words, when what I want is to leave

the literal entirely, my hands ending in ten
feathers, my mouth a simple net. . . . I pin

my arms to my sides and watch her word roots
shiver into sentences like something shot

in time-lapse—the handshake, maybe, begun
as earnest proof that no weapons

would be used, graduating
into surgery, sculpture, all the ways we sing.

Villa Maria

All day my mother has worked
at learning to walk and speak.
Soon she'll be wheeled outside,
sunlight chattering from the bright
spokes of the chair she hates,
her useless arm casually arranged
on the plastic tray.

Last night on her TV
a shaman in Mombasa wrote
words from the Koran on a white
plate with saffron ink,
then dissolved them in rosewater
to make his medicine.

Where I wait the trees
are a tenement of birds
grown fat on the pity of visitors.
All afternoon a robin,
harnessed to flight,
streaks through the tines of an oak
with scraps for its young.

When she comes, I'll report
what Father ate, read her the latest
batch of cards. She'll say
"playpen" for "radio" and call me

by my dead sister's name.
At dusk the robins will nest,
their orange breasts setting
like suns.

In Kenya, the holy man
will rise to face Mecca
and choose the text to be consumed.
As if pressed in the pages
of a book, Mother will sleep
between sheets smoothed by the nuns
whose voices I hear now,
soaring upward like wings
in search of the thermals.

Hydrotherapy

Between laps the sun drops
through its arc, lurching
like the clock hand
I secretly watched
during homeroom Bible reading,
certain only time, not prayer,
would take me to my Maker.
These days I am out of my element

everywhere. On airplanes
I strike foxhole bargains.
In the pool, I thrash out
drowning scenes: cramps
which roll me to a bowling
ball, aspirin-induced stroke
(face-down, top step),
or simple panic in the deep

end. I want to be light
as an oil slick. I want
to believe in the clearer
tensions, in Archimedes' laws.
He was searching for impure gold
in his king's new crown
when he discovered the principle
of displacement: a body in fluid grows

light. But it's an uneasy union—
water seeping into my goggles,
coarse threads of hair stitching
in and out of my mouth.
The principle of buoyancy
that keeps us all afloat
despite our faith or lack of it
sent the royal goldsmith

to his death.
Now my arms tick forward
freestyle, crossing the pool
seventy long times. I leave
no tracks and never arrive.
The swim lane deepens
with dusk. The sun
spills nothing as it sets.

Sestina for Indian Summer

October, and the kudzu still spreads
the pines and oaks with green
skirts wide as tents, still pairs
shack and shrub in a false
harmony, still resists the shave
of autumn's cool blade. Wait

for me like that. Wait
like heat rising under a spread
wing, like the cautious glide of a shaver
over skin or the slow greening
of bronze. Time is a false-
bottomed chest, a basket of pears

that never ripen, a clock pared
down to a single *tick*. Wait
as the orchard did, its false
rigging of blossoms spread
windward, then snagged on the green
slope where today tractors shave

the dropped leaves to dust. Say *a close shave,*
meaning you escaped a dangerous pair:
proximity and severance, green
belief and the final *no.* Wait
somewhere between the two, spreading
the words apart the way waterfalls

chisel through stone. The false
colors of autumn are summer's shavings,
bits of sun and lake spread
in the trees, fluttering above the pair
of lovers who recur but do not last. Wait
until they're replaced by the green

thrust of the kudzu, that greenery
that does not flame before it falls.
Seasons always bring the pasts we waited
for, when the calendar was shaved
to a strip narrow as a paring
of light glimpsed through a lover's spread

hand. We were the green pair who spread
the season thin, waiting and counting on
autumn's sheaves. We were the false summer.

Wanting His Child

All night I dreamed of ornate fountains,
water sprayed in intricate designs
like liquid lace or the traceries of Gothic
windows turned translucent, silver
under a full moon. And I watched the water
traveling toward this art—down
from clouds, up through capillary
grasses from the oceans, dipped from wells
by women whose scarves waved like kelp
in dyeing vats where water briefly
married earth's colors to the cloth
and then sluiced on. And I thought
how water's clarity was born:
of mountains worn to chimney and ravine,
of streams hatching egg-shaped gravel.
And of how far love takes us—farther
than water—to bridge the vast distance
between *him* and *her*:
the quiet trespass to a room,
the chasm in the throat a name
must leap across. Oh something in me clots,
something longs for form when he's inside me
and I want him there as long as he
can stay, until I'm drenched with pattern,
until we're flesh and thorn, the roar
of the stone lion whose mouth pours water
into the pool he guards, lighting small fires
in his own reflection.

The Naturalist's Ritual

It happens when you are in your boat,
the sea moving beneath you like a woman,
the sun in its breastplate daring you.
All the coins you ever wished on
school just below the surface.
You need to outrun them,
let the motor out until the torn
cloth of the wind lashes
your face. From the lens
of your beautiful eye,
upside-down, a picture moves
toward the brain: a man
chipping the waves to mica,
making the sea a hard thing.

For Those Saved in the Army-Navy Medical Museum

Paying for sundries at a country store
I bump a gallon jar of pickled
eggs, each slick white oval
moving aimless as a blind
eye, as the bottled fetuses
I saw as a girl at the Museum
on Sunday afternoons.

"Stages of Our Growth" was a room
full of interrupted babies,
old enough, had they lived,
to be my parents.
Sometimes I'd pretend
they were just waiting to play,
pressed against rain-slicked windowpanes.

The embryo at four weeks,
a pink tadpole fixed in plastic,
hung sweet as any locket
near the door. Twelve specimens away,
a full-term boy
had drifted through two wars
still too small for his wrinkles.

I was awed by the unfurling
of the spine, the arm knobs
bursting into stars,

fingernails coming on like a fine patina.
And anxious for my own wet machinery to begin:
for an egg to ripen and slide
down the anemone-fringed tube,

wafted toward the dark pear.
I think it was a kind of worship
when I shivered at those frail ones
weaned on formalin, a kind of love
I felt for the wells of the primitive eyes,
the organs veiled
like bruises by the skin.

At a certain stage you got sex
and fingerprints, the folds and whorls
and clefts of what we are. Later,
that fetal expression appeared—something
like a smirk on those perfect lips—
that seemed to say *we are*
your open arms.

Romantic, at Horseshoe Key

All day the light breaks up the waves,
turning them over in dark spadefuls

while I fish from the pier raised
like a spyglass into the Gulf.

There is such eloquence in the factual
that has no name, in all the ways water

is patterned in a boat's wake: Laces
coming undone? A chain slipping its gears?

What should I call the time we ate cherries
by the pound for moisture, the water jug

forgotten on the dock? You said *years
from now our trees will crown this plot*

of water. A surf of blossoms,
our hands branded red as hearts. . . .

I can't subtract you from this place,
from the boat basin's curved

embrace, the red channel markers
that ripen all night in my sleep.

My pale purple line enters the water
and deflects like a censored

thought. Now I see you in your boat
moving quickly through the ink

of my poem. Gulls keep turning
the pages of the sky. I write

the way a shore bird prints her words
in sand to be read by water.

I name it romantic, this belief
that pain is only the bad year of an orchard.

First Day of the Season

Tonight, picking shot from their breasts,
I'll see the quail scatter again
in the pattern of their wounds.

Now it's up and over sapling
pine and sweetgum, the roll bar
holding like a crucial seam,

flannel whips of dog fennel
stickered to our clothes.
Sunrise welds the puddles

together with gold. Only an hour ago
there was the depthless black
you can't see through the city's cataracts:

not a human backdrop, but a reason
for the self to settle its own blank terrain.
Starlight held these men like a thin cocoon

until they awoke, transformed,
and gently took their guns down
from racks. The one I came with

sounds as if he's going to cry
each time the dogs point game,
his voice quivering at the shrill pitch

where delight and terror overlap,
where the lost sailor warbles,
marking a leaf on water,

and the broker abstracts
destiny from a ticker tape.
He stands straight up in the jeep,

hoists his gun and it's like
seeing again after being blind,
sighting down the barrel: coveys

flushing like fireworks, his father
swinging a fox-tailed squirrel,
a buck twinned in the stream.

Deeper in these woods than we will go
he claims there's a night hunter,
a bird who pairs for life

whose only notion of himself
is a furious flicker
in the tiny eyes of his mate.

Synecdoche for Many Men

Lips full as hybrid roses,
the cock with its myriad
names and sly disguises,
sweet furrow at the hip?
No. I choose the breast
over which men exercise
little care or control—
nipples like vestigial
scars of swordplay,
areoles bristling at each
kiss. It is all I want
to do now—touch there
as if to prove we are
the same, suck a little
to see if anything softens,
work my lips and tongue
across the shallow bowl
where the ribs are spliced
to rouse the organ lodged
there, like a stone.

Floating Islands

The afternoon we swam nude
in the Gulf, the sun struck against the sky
like a brand slowly cooling,
the waves twinging apart as if they'd
learned modesty, I wanted to touch
his hips tapering in the murky
depth, and pick up the white shells
of his feet. I wanted my breasts
to bob free of the sea's plunging
neckline and taste his salty hair
and push it back and kiss his forehead and kiss
underwater on the lips, our breath
rising like columns of mercury,
his arms drifting around me
like strands of kelp. I wanted the water
to slow down his desire, I'd said,
so he'd know how a woman feels it,
more like a feather drawn
across the flesh than a flame. For an hour
we floated, two shy camellias
in a shallow blue bowl. We talked
and treaded and kept our distance.
But that night in the shower he pressed
one of his legs between mine and asked
could I pee right then so he'd know the slow
warm sensation down a woman's thighs.

Fugue

It happens at the supermarket,
he is buying
a loaf of bread with a stone
mill on the wrapper
and the waterwheel begins to churn
the cellophane
and raise the hair on his neck.
Through the cart's fence-wire,
wild phlox, then cattle
arrayed on the pasture like musical notes.
He cups his hands
to his face to inhale the smell
of a life in the fields, but instead
of embedded earth, there is only
the shadow of a window
awning. *The thick sponge*
of moss between the stones . . . water
rushing and plinking. How long
has he been standing
here like a lawn jockey
on which someone has thoughtfully
painted clothes and a face?

In the car, rays of sun
fall like splinters
from a saw. Beside him, on the seat,
a headline: "Muscle jobs move

to Singapore, the Pacific
rim." His own hands could be
anything—the figural tops
of urns, worms. A man
when he awakes is more like a story
than flesh: it doesn't matter
where he has slept or whether
he lies.
                The sun keeps beating down
like an untranslated curse,
coming closer for maybe a thousand
years. In the rear-view mirror
his face simplifies and flattens
like a figure in a cartouche:
Here is the head of a jackal,
here are vulture's wings,
in pure profile,
which means a going away.
Here is the traffic he weaves through
sharp as a scream.

I Picture You at Your Piano

For D.M.

Tonight, hearing Chopin,
I picture you at your piano
as a young man,
the eighty-eight keys
distinct as nations
and your hands stately
diplomats. It is the moment
before the music comes.
You unlatch the metronome
that will rest like a small
coffin atop a larger one
after the sawmill
takes four fingers.
But now it lolls at *legato*
as if your whole future
could be spanned by a hand
practiced in languor.
You play for an hour,
a fever on your cheeks
as you invoke
the noble peasantry—
that bouquet of bare
shoulders, red ribbons swift
as grace notes in their hair.
You will forever after
be a romantic
and though you'll never

leave the small town
of your birth, you'll travel far
into exile like Chopin
and burn for lost causes
and believe more in the silences
of the world
than its sounds.

Among the Cows

Advised to breathe with the Holsteins
     as a form of meditation,
I open a window in my
     mind and let their vast humid breath,
sticky flanks, the mantric switching
     of their tails drift through. I lie down
with them while they crop the weedy
     mansions, my breasts muffled like the
snouts of foxes run to ground. I
     need to comfort the cows, the way
heart patients stroke cats and the grief
     of childhood is shed for dogs. I
offer them fans of grass under
     a sky whose grey may be the hide
of some huge browser with sun and
     moon for wayward eyes. It begins

to rain. How they sway, their heavy
     necks lift and strain. Then, like patches
of night glimpsed through a bank of clouds,
     they move toward four o'clock, the dark
fragrant stalls where dawn will break first
     as the curved pink rim of their lips.
I want to believe I could live
     this close to the earth, could move with
a languor so resolute it
     passes for will, my heart riding

low in my body, not this flag
      in my chest snapped by the lightest
breeze. Now my breath escapes with theirs
      like doused flames or a prayer made
visible: May our gender bear
      us gracefully through in these cumbrous frames.

II

Pope Joan

*Being Documents Found on the Body of Pope John VIII**

I. To Those Who Shall Discover Me

I have no story but the origins
of things: see how my quill
even as I write, suddenly lifts
in the air, remembering it was wing
before it was pen.

Now you shall distrust everyone.

Now even the building acquires
gender—arch and passageway
frankly coupled in daylight,
the rain coursing through the gutters
sexual, the garden obscene.

The mystery is deeper
than the Mass. Once I desired
the slur of the vernacular
in my ear, evening untrussed
and spilling like a cornucopia,
my hair stroked, breasts
unbound until urgency pressed

---

*Pope Joan, according to most sources, began her career as an ecclesiastic scribe. She joined
a Benedictine monastery at the insistence of her first lover and later moved to Athens and
Rome, where, still disguised as a man, she became cardinal and then, in 856, pope. She was
stoned to death in 858, after giving birth during a papal procession.*

piety itself
into my flesh by slow accretion
like the making of lace
or the way time stitches the bones
of animals onto stone.
No. Nothing so cleanly chiseled.
Picture my grace, instead,
as the empty spot
in this altarpiece if tonight
the Virgin, perpetually fixed
in the painter's blue
were to slip
the gold bars of her frame, away
from all that radiance.

In this gravel beneath my feet,
mountains. In this taper,
the hot breath and slick hide
of something once alive.
I have read in *Luke* where Adam
is called Son of God
and declare myself Daughter,
my child equally blessed.
Now let the censers swing.
Let the voices chime the name
of my successor.

II. After Love

Let me not be turned into a dove
like St. Gertrude. I do not wish
to fly away. Already my breasts
like two soft pigeons have nested
in the cup of his hands. Let me not

be bedecked
with a virgin's beard or pluck
out my eyes like St. Lucy
because I am part of the beauty
of the world. Let my face bloom

in the cowl
like a crocus breaking through
the cold dark soil
of winter. Let the dust always
look this golden, let me stay

in this place,
commanding the hours like a breviary.
If he shuns my cell, let it
temper me, like the icy
stream at Meinengen where I

was baptized
and the swordsmiths plunged their new
blades.

III. Hymn

I welcome this child who'll come
into the world crying
his father's sharp cry
of delight, his father
whose mouth closed first
over these nipples when love
led him all the way back
to himself, before language
or judgment. Afterwards, I studied

his body like the pattern books
of shells and *rinceaux* and strapwork
that illumine the holy words—
downy arms shone like two
bold flourishes in gold leaf,
rungs of sinew and muscle
sprang up between his ribs
with each deep breath—the ladder
to heaven is within us!

I pitied the monks in their cassocks
like stinking dromedaries,
their heads lowered
to the rough boards, an iron spoon
or buffalo-horn cup parting their lips.

36

Or at night in their cells,
undressing in a cloud of garlic
and lice, the black soutane by the bed
waiting to baffle the dawn.

I wanted to sing my lover's
praises, I wanted to wear anklets
of bells and perform
a prayer with my feet.
So many crucifixions around us
and we bejeweled with sweat.
We were the scribes who sang aloud
the verses we copied,
we made the elbows push out

the word *holy*. We pulled
the cords of the thighs
until bells pealed. If I spend
the rest of my days kneeling
on cold stone floors,
if I have to water dry staves
until they flower and bathe in ashes
and flog myself with the taws,
inside me there will still be this

unfolding.

IV. Elegy

O lift the tiny feet and hands, lift
the head carefully as a jug of wine, as blown
glass. Rinse the eyes clear. Part and comb
the fine hair, and in the desk drawer sift
among the clutter for the small gold
crucifix to be worn around his neck—a rose
of Sharon, its blossoms raging against the base
of the cross. Be wary of drafts and cold
linens. Remember when you walk, he's not safely
tucked inside like a foot curled away from a fire,
but rides noisily upon your arm, precariously
upon your arm. Glide like a blade of light! The air,
the sunny air which polishes his cheeks and fills
his eyes with sky cannot catch him if he falls.

V. Sestina of Visions

Tonight, after evening prayers, I saw the nuns
leaving church, spilling out like the black
beads of a broken rosary. Twilight had hung orange ribbons
in the trees and embers glowed in every pane
of glass, so that it seemed they passed through a chaste
fire, their breath steaming like a noiseless pealing

of bells. Hell must be the red of the peeled
slice of sun that smoldered at their feet. The nuns
say they've seen the color of heaven in the chased
gold chalice of the Mass. I imagine a perfect black-
ness where passions rest like eyes behind a dark pane. . . .
Starlings swooped above them, the invisible ribbons

that bind earth and sky in their beaks, the same ribbons
that slowly streak through rocks. Father, I love to peel
the appleskin unbroken and find, uncoiling like pain,
a bright red snake dangling from my knife. O nuns,
my sisters, do you love the fiery sky or must you blacken
the lilies with faith and lay over everything a chaste

grey pall? At midnight, a dream: a demon chased
me with a copper comb to flay my flesh to ribbons.
If I swallowed enough stones, relishing them like black-
berries, I grew light enough to fly. Pebbles pealed

from my hands and mouth, my belly swelled like a nun's
apron dancing on the line. I had to take pains

not to float entirely away. . . . I awoke with pain
in my legs, an animal hobbled by an unchaste
burden. Can I escape my fate if my nun-
cio proclaims the birth miraculous—the rib bone
of the Pope fashioned into a child? I see blood pealing
onto cobblestones, my robes torn off, blackened

by the waters. As Venice seems to melt when its black
lagoons are glazed with sun, so when my pains
come, Rome shall burn. They say it feels like being peeled
from the inside out, sawed in half like the chaste
St. Julitta, whose blood flowed in sleek ribbons
that spelled the name of God. I have lost my soul. Tell the nuns

to beware: pain is the ribbon tied around pleasure. All births
are chaste. If heaven is repealed because I ruled not nuns
but men, I will celebrate the other, the Black Mass.

III

From the Wailing Wall

It's an ordinary rock
without a single elegant edge,
a dolt of a rock
unlike the arrowheads
we've found in streams,
those nimbly chinked blades
that cleave the light
with one purpose.
This rock hoards shadows
in its pocked surface.
We place it next to our other books
as if it were the fossil
record of prayer,
an unsplit geode
with ancient words
glittering at its core.

Soon the bit of rubble rules
the house, paring all our goods
down to mannerisms, ploys.
It is the weed in the garden
of history, what must be swept
again and again from doorsills,
the part of the outside
that keeps wanting in.
It is the muscle of the land.
If there is another world

this is its scaffolding—
what comes to hand
from the hard earth
for building or throwing
under our blue
curfew, the sky.

At Dawn

These days he uses no alarm clock
and claims the sun rises as a hot ache

in his joints, his bones grown hollow,
barometric as a bird's. He knows

there is a chance that he will die—
the arm going numb, the vertigo when he rises.

He's worshipping each time he bends or twists
suddenly, each time he checks his wrist—

the pulse like a fern ticking on glass—
as if god could be plied with what is dangerous.

His god is small and was tractable once before.
It was June 1941, in a depot east of Warsaw.

His mother had climbed down to the platform
searching for food when smoke swarmed

along the tracks, a tunnel of ash
billowing in place of the train on which

she'd left her infant son. What else
could have carried her scream with the force

of a command to the indifferent ears
of the engineer, the word *Stop!* soaring. . . .

Now, in this pre-dawn light, the birds
in the Audubon print above the bed emerge

as they did 160 years ago: a pair
of blue-winged teal barely

distinct from the shrouded Newfoundland
coast they sail over, wings half-folded,

the orange speckled breast of the male
the first real evidence of day. In the pale

moments before he wakes, I imagine
sketching them from life, groping for crayon

pencil, pastel, shading the bright blue epaulets
of the shoulders, glossing the beaks with eggwhite

though in fact the artist wired fresh skins
in dynamic poses and even then

had to race to achieve the delicate hues
of the eyes and feet which were always

the first to fade, his art less in the drawn
image than in the vigil he kept, in the dawns

he lifted like veils, in observing the lines
of a face over and over until he captured

the living likeness of the bird.

Bypass

For A, after surgery

The respirator swayed and rose like a hooded
cobra from your mouth while the scrub
nurse squeezed the black rubber bulb
that held your breath after two dead
hours on the heart-lung machine. If love
was the slow growth of something like a membrane
between us, illness was the knife that severed
that bridge, separated the Siamese twins.
We don't even want to forget the same things:
you, the pain clawing through a thick
narcotic haze; I, everything they wouldn't let
me see—ribs sprung like binder rings,
the heart delivered on its cords, slick
and still as a baby before its first breath.

On Jekyll Island

The remains of the Horton-Dubignon Plantation

The marker says "Tabby Ruin"
   and we get out of the car to see
      the unstoppered walls,

a hearth shaped like a mouthful
   of ashes. Overhead, the sky
      pours in like history,

so much light, so little
   form. "Tabby" was the local
      concrete, a porridge

of sand and shells dug from Indian
   mounds. Everywhere the stucco
      has flaked, oyster shucks

claw toward us, the hands
   of slaves who bent to the Sea
      Island cotton

that foamed up in this marsh
   like a hundred-year tide.
      I have been reading about the Grand

Tours of the Europeans: they loved
   to be photographed jauntily
      posed with classical

ruins. A century before the camera,
   they painted the fantasy: afternoon
      picnics in a tame

wood, a small orchestra playing,
   the minuet danced before
      broken Roman columns.

Here the Africans sang of thorn
   plants that would bleed
      the color from their

skin. Most of them never set foot
   in this house that now feels less
      somebody's home

than a temple where weather
   is part of the worship
      and the accidental is taken

for fate. Even in the painting
   where the shot stag is propped
      among acanthus

leaves and the gentlemen ride
   a fallen pediment,
      their stockinged calves

the same incandescent peach
   as the sky, the eye is drawn
      finally

upward, to the only monumental
   they or we are sure of—
      the clouds moving by like worn

signets, though we never touch
   them, though we know them only
      from pages and pages of rain.

To the Field of Reeds

Look now, the guide says, at the story
from the tomb of the scribe, Ani.

Accused of too studious a life, in the frieze
above my head Ani gains heaven because

his heart passed the test. But first, reclined
on a slant board, he's gutted and drained

and packed in natron to stop the rot.
The husks of two crocodiles and a pet

cat, all bound in linen, accompany him
to the Afterlife—not the stuffy room

they found him in, heaped up with booty,
but a small desk stocked with dyes

and inks and a pair of palm fans to sway
over his two ghosts—the one who'll stay

in his body, fingering the quill pen,
the barley and wine, and the one,

more like our souls, who'll wander far from home
as I do now in the British Museum

where I witness the trial of Ani's
heart: separately

preserved, placed on golden scales,
it's weighed against a feather to settle

his final fate. Will the two totter, equal
as dry leaves on a wave? Or must his heart be full

of feeling, heavy with passions, for Ani to cross
to the Field of Reeds?

But look! It rises, light
as a grain of pollen or this surprising thought—

that paradise measures not pain or duty or even love,
those trophies saved in the heart, but what we can give

up. In the last panel, beside Osiris's throne,
see how the vacant-hearted scribe takes to the divine,

conversing with the half-mad,
the half-animal gods?

Shards

Inside the strict pine coffin
he is wrapped
in a cotton sheet
and over the three vanities—
the eyes and mouth—
potsherds have been placed.
All night a vigilant Jew
sat by the body
while a candle ate
into the dark
and his feet grew rigid
pointing to Jerusalem.
Now we cover him

with tidewater clay.
To slow us down,
to remind us that grief
is a difficult labor, we dig
at first with shovels
turned over, a trickle
of red dirt fine
as hourglass sand.
Then we are permitted
grunting shovelfuls, stabs
that match the cries

of the mourners who watch
from unsteady chairs
as we spade respect
onto the *aron,*
Hebrew for coffin, for clothes closet,
wardrobe, chest of drawers,
that one word conveying
what we hope against:
that nothing can contain us,
that wood itself
is only soil haunting
the above-ground world,

ghosts in solid form.
It is right that burial
begin at the face
with earth baked
into something like a memory
of itself,
so that his humanness
can be taken away from us,
so we will not picture him
about to blink or speak,
so we may begin the leveling
with small rubble.

Freestyle, on the First of Tishri

The metaphor here is the pool, regular
and deep as the tradition itself. First I float,
still and buoyant in what I don't
accept. Then I shatter the surface, a scholar
dissecting text not to destroy but to enrich,
a farmer plowing and disking the earth
before planting. On land, I forget breath's
noisy ball bearings, the flutter kick's
fringes blazing like tangible will. I imagine
that faith is nothing but a grudging promise
of repetition, like these laps, until this
continual splash in the mind begins—
not with grievance or prayer
but as gasp, a momentary bargain struck with the air.

Learning CPR

The dummies, all named Annie, all without hearts,
arrive in blue valises, their faces scuffed like soles
of shoes. Powerful coil springs
in their chests resist like bone when the clear
plastic lungs inflate. A box like a small
traffic signal lights up to show if the help

we give is: (red) breaking a rib; (green) helping
her breathe; (yellow) reviving the pulse. The heart
can stop for six minutes before small
deaths in the brain carry off the soul
as we know it: speech, movement, a clear
memory we can dip into like a spring-

fed well. We kneel like runners ready to spring
at the gun. But before the heroics, before we help,
we make sure Annie hasn't fainted or isn't clearing
her mind with simple sleep the way a hart
might clear a stone wall, bounding as the soul
would if it could travel apart from its small

carrying case, the body. "Annie! Annie!" our small
voices cry from all corners, tightening the springs
in our thighs. We slap her, lightly, solely
because it's required. We say, "Somebody go for help,"
to the blank walls, the vinyl face, the heartless
floor. I picture a doctor screaming, "CLEAR!"

then the paddles, the needle jumping clear
off the scale. We place our palms in the small
space above the sternal notch, the heart's
door latch, bounce fifteen times on Annie's bedsprings,
then, mouth-to-mouth, two breaths, a large helping
of air while we pinch the nostrils shut so the soul

won't escape. Few of us believe in the soul.
It's a word we never use, though its meaning is clear
tonight: the uncomposed face of the helpless;
the person inside us who emerges in the small
hours of a crisis; the handsprings
we turn to find love in the world; the heart

outside our hearts. We're clearing Annie's airway
balanced on small knees, using elbows for springs,
hearing our souls cry *Call 911. Help me. Please.*

Into the Motion of Other Things

There's a lamp clamped to my desk and on its blue
enamel shade the overhead fan, reflected
as a tiny pinwheel, spins as if to show
how the atoms inside must move—electrons
orbiting, smaller agitated particles
slamming and humming within the thick
metal cone, like the traffic of blood cells
just beneath the skin. Outside, leaves quake
on stilled twigs, soil heaves up, grain
by grain. Grit floats on the tide of my eye,
today's excuse to grieve for you, gone now,
not into stillness, but into the motion
of other things, like the water that spilled
as the child carried it to you in her hands.

The Suit Too Small, the Words

My father gives my son the black
suit he wore for his golden anniversary,
after emphysema reduces him
to 102 pounds of rack
and flaccid skin, grumbling
sticks and stones. He always fired
words like weapons, the belt
he used to blister me, wasn't it just
the servant of his tongue?

Now he shuffles through tropical rooms,
his face the yellow of old
tabloids, fist crumpled
around the nebulizer he sucks on
all day long. His suit fits
my son for a year, then hangs
in the hall closet behind my winter skirts,
soaking up darkness.
One night three years later

I try it on myself, admiring
the fine weave, razor creases,
the breast pocket, feudal,
so exactingly stitched
that suddenly I think
breast pockets must have begun
as little shields for the heart,

the handkerchief pulled to a point
like a white flag.

I am lanky as he is, but taller.
The suit is much too small.
I consider alterations, Goodwill,
then return the suit to its plastic bag.
A day passes, two,
before I call. He complains
about his lungs, his income
tax, the weather. I can see
his coffee-colored lips

grazing the phone, his wavy hair
gleaming like polished steel.
I can hear the emphysema
blowing him up like a leaky
balloon. I know he's twisting
the gold ring my sister and I gave him
for his eightieth birthday—
the head of a thoroughbred, dimensional
through a pavé horseshoe wreath,

his big winner at last, waiting now
for the gambler to cross
the finish line. A feeling begins
inside me, rising like a swell

across water. I try
to push it back, I try to raise
my head above it like a swimmer
bobbling through a wave,
but I can see the suit from where I talk:

pleats, darts, shoulder pads,
lapels. It had touched
his body with joy.
It had held him up before me
like the little doll on wedding cakes:
Here is this man in black,
here is your father, unbending,
with his coward's heart and his rages,
which for some time now you have noticed

in yourself. You wanted the suit
to fit, not for sentimental
reasons, but to seal that awful bond,
to set your face like a moon
above that dark horizon and feel
the sorrow and brooding innate
as gravity's pull, the black
of the suit not a color but the darkness
that collects in an empty mold.

The words rise up, I can't help myself,
I tell him I love him
for the first time in my life.
He answers *I love you, too.*
Then silence, applied like a tourniquet
along 350 miles of cable and wire.
Then my own breathing, faint,
like the rustle you sometimes think
you hear when you are pushing through

a closet—some garment swaying
on its own, a prom dress, maybe,
your adolescence tatted in its lace.
I'll save the suit for a great-grandson,
like a Southerner proud of an ancestor's
Confederate grey. No. Like the uncle
I once saw crouch and bark
in the Japanese uniform
he tore from a Pacific beach.

You'd need to slip inside the enemy's skin,
to pray, like the primitive,
to the totem of the animal you hunted
who might have killed you first.
But I do not want to eat his heart.
I want to give it back to him,
saying *something always suffices*

as love. That is the worst flaw
in the design, that we come to love

our captors.
    Now I have the suit,
too small, an impractical memento,
his dark moods spreading in me,
and the words we spoke,
deleted so long from our lives
that they have no context
beyond the soft nap of virgin wool,
a vacant sleeve.

The Last Father Poem

As if by a raptor
who cradles under his dark
scapulars the small prey
he culled from the field,
you are lifted out now,
his pinions shifting
and settling like black
shantung. You are held
in the scrimshaw beak,
reduced to a fleck
in the agate eyes, then
released into the blind
grass. The grief is that
unnatural, that tame.

Refusing the Call

For Henry Roth, author of Call It Sleep

It's said you spoke once and then chose silence,
a waterfowl farm in Maine. Did the loft
of snow and feathers white out the violence
of the Lower East Side? The Maine coast sifts
light, explains horizons, while the city stirs
strange magic in a child: a patch of sun that creeps
between the tenements, the ruby flare
of rosary beads. Once you saw high voltage leap
between train tracks and feared it was the word
of God. He chose you, but you called it *sleep*.
In Maine, touched by their sameness, you killed the birds
yourself. I imagine you saw portents seep
from the runnels of bloody snow, that the cambered
blade felt heavy in your hand as slumber.

The Dig at Caesarea Maritima

Caesarea Maritima, an ancient seaport south of Haifa, was built by Herod in 13 B.C.E. The object of repeated battles, it was conquered and destroyed for the final time in 1291.

Gulls have plundered this beach
for centuries, nesting among relics
left by Turks and Crusaders, legal
stelae of Byzantine kings, traces
of Rome. Salt water ages a generation
ancient in months, so most of what I sift

is garbage. Still I tunnel and sift
among the French safes, bottles, beach
tar—all the cast-offs of my generation
which, like this harbor and its derelict
ships, sink into the future. I trace
ten razings, Muslim heads sold illegally

as trophies, Crusaders flayed by legal
mandate of the sultan. The sword's siftings
were always crude. Across the ridged traces
of high tide I drag my spade. The beach
erases easily, its surface a relic
delicate as onionskin where waves generate

patterns that repeat like genes or the ratio
of *pi*. Digging teaches this: the legal
part of any slaughter is the relic
used—the labyrs, gun, train. . . . Sifting
in Herod's palace, where the beach
swallowed his pool, I found traces

of his patronage—lead tokens traced
with a wheat plume, a kind of degenerate
money. The real Roman coin, a sword beached
in rusty sand—red flakes like hard legal
proof of old bloodshed—set my sifter
chattering with bits of bone, relics

too small to display. Their only reliquary
will be a laboratory slide, the traces
of diet and disease light sifts
from biopsies. I dig. I generate
artifacts in the name of History, the first legal
invader here. But the gulls who comb the beach

carried off its story in their beaks, generations
sifting relics to feed their young every trace
of the legal tender of this beach, the dead.

The Uncommon Hours

Driving I-95 at night,
passing pasture and pond,
I think of that friendly iconoclast,
Thoreau, and wonder
what he would make
of this broad scratch
in the land. Would it suffice
as a modern "stroll
upon the beach
as near the ocean's edge
as [he] could go?"
Wouldn't he park the car

and, flashlight in hand,
walk across the dark field
toward a life he'd call
"unexpected in common hours"—
past cattle pitched
like tents in the grass,
through the oak hammock
and into the panther's den?
The egrets would have lost
their whiteness
and the bluebird
that "carries the sky on his back"

darkened under that weight.
Would he split a blade
of grass with his teeth?
Listen while the wind
scours the dark mouths
of the trees? Saddened
by the earth's capacity
for loss, wouldn't he still
want what all of us want—
to cross the field first
without conscience
and then as pure voice?

Notes

Page 4:
This poem owes some of its inspiration and structural strategies to Deborah Digges's poem "Laws of Falling Bodies."

Pages 36–37:
In "Hymn," lines 30–31 and 40–44 are taken loosely from Emmanuel Royidis's *Pope Joan,* translated and adapted by Lawrence Durell.

Page 55:
The First of Tishri is the Jewish New Year.